Savor the Savior

For Kids

Bible, Pencil, Sundae!

Jeri R. Daniel

Savor the Savior for Kids by Jeri R. Daniel
Copyright © 2011 by Jeri R. Daniel
All Rights Reserved.
ISBN: 978-1-59755-270-7

Published by: ADVANTAGE BOOKS™
Longwood, Florida
www.advbookstore.com

Library of Congress Control Number: 2011932361

Cover design by Pat Theriault

First Printing: July 2011
11 12 13 14 15 16 17   10 9 8 7 6 5 4 3 2 1
Printed in the United States of America

Dedication

This book is dedicated to my Heavenly Father, Who loves me as His child, and to the children He has given me to love: Amy, Lisa, Kara, Angie, Lydia, and Kaleb.

Endorsements

"It has been said that darkness is constantly chasing us. If we are spiritually idle, the ways of the world will not only catch us, but will also catch the next generation! If you want to pass the baton of Truth to your kids and their kids, this book will give you both a jump start and a practical plan for any age to impact the world immediately and when they graduate from high school! Whoever wants the next generation more will get them...do you?"

Nathan Wilder
Minister of Students and Sports Outreach
First Baptist Church Oviedo, FL

"Parents have been given an awesome responsibility to train up their children in the nurture and admonition of the Lord. However, it seems today that parents, including Christian parents, are more concerned with raising up a child that is well rounded socially and academically. If they even think on the spiritual side, it is just to make sure their children will get to go to heaven. I am so encouraged by Jeri Daniel's book *Savor the Savior for Kids*, which puts the emphasis where it belongs, making sure that your child has a personal relationship with Christ and that they know how to maintain that relationship on a daily basis. Every parent would benefit by having this book as a part of their family curriculum."

Barry Edwards
Minister of Children
First Baptist Church Oviedo, FL

"Jeri has generously shared her personal experience in discovering the value and importance of teaching a child how to use a prayer journal. You will find she provides clear guidance on the tools and methods you can use to help lay a foundation for your child to develop a life-long desire for conversations with the Lord. As you are given a glimpse into her own children's journals, you will even better understand how a child can worship God through this daily interaction. Her enthusiasm for including kids in what others might consider something just for "grown-ups" will encourage you to get started with your children... regardless of their age!"

Debbie Valle
Director of Preschool Ministries
First Baptist Church Oviedo, FL

Acknowledgments

I thank Christ. I am clinging to You for the ride of my life!

Ron Daniel, you are the perfect Daddy for our kids! Thank you for sharpening each one of those arrows to be shot out into the world. What an adventure life is together!

Amy, Lisa, Kara, Angie, Lydia, and Kaleb, Daddy and I love you so very much, and God loves you way more! Thank you for proofreading, feasting and growing in Jesus, and sharing your special prayer journals, so others can know His love, too.

To my church family, First Baptist Church of Oviedo, thank you for your prayers, support, and encouragement.

I am forever grateful to each and every one who helped to feed me spiritually at any given time in my life. You know who you are. Thanks to all who prayed for the books and the ministry.

Thank you to Melba and Dave Daniel for choosing to jump on this ride with us! How God has blessed us through the generations before us! He knew all along, didn't He?

Mom, (Nana, Bebe) you are my constant cheerleader and source of godly counsel. I am blessed beyond measure to call you my mom *and* my sister in Christ. "I scream, 'Son Days!'" was a great idea!

Thank you to Carolyn D. Phillips for proofreading and to Lyn Nelson, Nathan Wilder, Barry Edwards, and Debbie Valle for the content review.

Mike and Karen Janiczek and Pat Therriault, thank you for everything.

Table of Contents

SECTION ONE

SUMMARY/OVERVIEW

I Scream, "Son Days Every Day!"

<u>Savor the Savior for Kids</u> will teach you a variety of ways to introduce delicious spiritual food to your children, from toddlers to tweens to teens. ***Like creating the ideal ice cream sundae, you will discover the perfect enticing combination for each of your children to grow in Christ.*** Can you keep from smiling as you watch a kid eagerly pile on the sundae toppings and then delight in every bite? Just wait for the joy that comes from seeing a child delight in the Lord in such a way, and then top that with the fruit of the Spirit! Through daily conversations with God, they will "Taste and see that the Lord is good!"

Jeri Daniel

SECTION TWO

INTRODUCTION

The Perfect Recipe

Daily journal writing with children has been one of the highlights of all my teaching experiences. From kindergarten teacher to homeschool mom, the rewards from those precious interactions are priceless. Averaging thirty students per kindergarten class, and now with six of my own to homeschool, I especially love the stolen few minutes of quality time with each individual.

In public school, one beaming child after another would come up to my desk to proudly share that special paper. As the eager author/artist told me about the penciled picture or read the misspelled words, I would quickly add to the paper exactly what was dictated. Immediately, I would tell how proud I was and encourage the child to "read" what I had written. Since it had just come from his or her own mouth, there was no struggle to decipher each word. Twinkling eyes and broad grins confirmed the self-satisfaction as the next student took a turn. What prizes these papers formed as we continued the routine throughout the school year and sent them home as a book! Each page showed such progress!

Once homeschooling, I implemented only the curriculum and methods from public school which had proven to be successful in my experience. I had been given the opportunity to teach reading and writing using a wide variety of techniques in order to meet the needs of many different learning styles and abilities. My favorite and most successful approach has always been journal writing. It covers phonics and sight words, reading silently, reading aloud, writing, and the subject matter for the journal entry. Regular journal writing also allows for the creativity of artwork and for each unique personality to blossom unhindered.

In the beginning, my children's journals represented their own "daily news" of what was happening that day. It consisted of adorable descriptions of *extremely* important topics like: "what we ate for lunch" or "how mommy needs a nap." *(Some things never change.)* As we added in more kiddos to the homeschool classroom mix, I periodically adjusted as the ages and stages and needs evolved.

When my fourth daughter joined the ranks, it was one too many "plates" to juggle, and they all seemed to come crashing down at once. The number of students increased, but I still had the same fixed amount of time. What could I possibly do? In my quest to reduce the sheer number of individual lessons, I combined as many subjects and age groups as possible. Why couldn't Bible reading be combined with journal writing? I, myself, had kept a prayer journal for years. It just had never occurred to me to try it for all the ages of my kids. What did I have to lose? One of the beauties of homeschooling is that I typically get the principal's approval to try new things, since he is my husband. He approved.

Since then, we have added to our schooling another daughter and a son. These two kiddos have regularly used their prayer journals since they were two years old. Impossible? Not at all. Included in this book are "free samples" from each stage, ages two to sixteen. Just as there are many different ways to make the perfect ice cream sundae, there are a variety of possible styles to use in the prayer journals. Some entries are very simple (think plain vanilla with a cherry on top) and others include a little of everything (ice cream, syrups, candies, nuts, whip cream, sprinkles, and a cherry). Look through the pages ahead to find the perfect recipe for each of your children.

Jeri Daniel

SECTION THREE

MATERIALS

Set the Table for Spiritual Dessert

I use the cheapest ***composition notebook*** that I can find. They are easy to locate. Most drugstores and grocery stores carry them (and sometimes the dollar stores, too). I prefer to have my kids use a ***pencil*** with a good ***eraser*** to prevent frustration if there are mistakes. As they get older, some may switch to ***ink pens for different colors. Crayons*** and ***colored pencils*** are great to have handy for additional artwork on the page, but avoid markers, which bleed through the pages. Use a ***real Bible*** for all ages—yes, even toddlers. I love to use ***The Beginner's Bible*** storybook as a supplement with the younger kids, but not as a replacement to the Bible. Keep everything together for easy daily access in your child's special "spot" for conversations with God. *The efficiency of set up and clean up often determines the quality and quantity of the quiet time.*

SECTION FOUR

PREPARATION

Accept the Invitation

In order to enjoy that special ice cream sundae party, someone must first buy the ingredients and invite others to share them. Without accepting the invitation, there will be no dessert to enjoy. What a waste of all that was purchased! For children old enough to understand the offer, they may answer for themselves with, "No, thank you," or, "Yes, please," and then go on to fix their sundaes without assistance. Younger ones may need a little help dishing up. It might even get messy! The littlest children will not understand the invitation at all, but there is no doubt that they will delight in getting tastes from those willing to share with them. Eventually, they, too, will grow to understand God's invitation, answer Him, and share the blessings with others.

Here I am! I stand at the door and knock. If anyone hears my voice and opens the door, I will come in and eat with that person, and they with me. Revelation 3:20

This verse is our personal offer from God to share His special gift: Himself. Eating with someone is a time of fellowship and conversation. Oh, how God wants to spend sweet time with each of us! How do we "open the door" for Him to come in? By answering Him when we understand that He is "knocking" or calling us to Him. *We are to thank Him for buying us the gift of life, ask for His forgiveness for our sins, and then join Him for our life party!*

> **For it is with your heart that you believe and are justified, and it is with your mouth that you profess your faith and are saved.** Romans 10:10

If your child has already accepted God's free invitation to "dine with Christ," then God's Spirit resides within that child's heart. If he or she is not yet to the point of understanding, then continue to offer morsels of God's truth, which will develop a taste for Him. Like a baby at an ice cream party, little bites that are sweet and easy to swallow will grow a desire for more.

> **Love the LORD your God with all your heart and with all your soul and with all your strength. These commandments that I give you today are to be on your hearts. Impress them on your children. Talk about them when you sit at home and when you walk along the road, when you lie down and when you get up.** Deuteronomy 6:5-7

> **Start children off on the way they should go, and even when they are old they will not turn from it.** Proverbs 22:6

Before a baby is quite ready to walk, the parents enthusiastically encourage the little tyke to first stand, and then to take tiny steps while holding on to something. It is a light-hearted game played over time with rewards of applause and squeals. This motivates the baby to try harder. Eventually, those chubby, little legs build the necessary muscle to do the job, but the rest of the body must be ready, too, in order to balance during those toddling victory steps. What rejoicing there is when that big day finally arrives!

Before a child is quite ready to read, the parents and teachers enthusiastically encourage the young student to first recognize letters and sounds, and then to piece them together into small words. It is a light-hearted game played over time with rewards of applause and words of praise. This motivates the young student to try harder. Eventually, the skills have all been learned, but the application comes with time. One day it seems to finally "click." What rejoicing there is when that big day finally arrives!

Before God's child is quite ready to accept Him as "Boss" for life, the parents and teachers enthusiastically encourage the child by sharing Bible stories, memory verses, and Jesus songs. It is a light-hearted game played over time with rewards of sweet smiles and words of praise. This motivates the child to try harder. Eventually, the skills have all been learned, but the understanding comes with time. One day it seems to finally "click." What rejoicing there is when that big day finally arrives!

> *I tell you that in the same way there will be more rejoicing in heaven over one sinner who repents than over ninety-nine righteous persons who do not need to repent.* Luke 15:7

Once Christ is received, His Spirit will bring further understanding:

> *What we have received is not the spirit of the world, but the Spirit who is from God, so that we may understand what God has freely given us. This is what we speak, not in words taught us by human wisdom but in words taught by the Spirit, explaining spiritual realities with Spirit-taught words.* 1 Corinthians 2:12-13

Which Utensils Should I Use?

While there are many great resources for helping children to understand what it means to be a Christian, all share the same basics, which are included in this section. One of my favorite tools, which is available online, is the EvangeCube. It is both easy and entertaining to use for adults and children. The following truths are listed here as a reference for adults. They are not intended to be just methodically read to the child. Choose the right one for the right time just as you would the proper utensil.

Sin is anything we think, say, or do to disobey God.

> ***...But if you do not do what is right, sin is crouching at your door; it desires to have you, but you must rule over it.*** Genesis 4:7b

Sin keeps all of us away from God, because He is perfect (holy).

> ***for all have sinned and fall short of the glory of God,*** Romans 3:23

The punishment for sin is death, apart from God forever.

> ***For the wages of sin is death, but the gift of God is eternal life in Christ Jesus our Lord.*** Romans 6:23

Jesus is the only One Who has not ever sinned.

> ***God made him who had no sin to be sin for us, so that in him we might become the righteousness of God.*** 2 Corinthians 5:21

God created us in love to spend sweet time with Him.

God is faithful, who has called you into fellowship with his Son, Jesus Christ our Lord. 1 Corinthians 1:9

NOTE: Fellowship means friendship.

He made a way to cover up our sins, so that He can be close to us forever.

For God so loved the world that he gave his one and only Son, that whoever believes in him shall not perish but have eternal life. John 3:16

While we are alive on earth, God lets us choose if we accept His free gift to live closely with Him.

If you declare with your mouth, "Jesus is Lord," and believe in your heart that God raised him from the dead, you will be saved. Romans 10:9

When we ask God to send His Holy Spirit to live inside of us, He comes and stays with us forever.

If you then, though you are evil, know how to give good gifts to your children, how much more will your Father in heaven give the Holy Spirit to those who ask him! Luke 11:13

And hope does not put us to shame, because God's love has been poured out into our hearts through the Holy Spirit, who has been given to us. Romans 5:5

With His Holy Spirit living inside of us, we are to honor God.

Do you not know that your bodies are temples of the Holy Spirit, who is in you, whom you have received from God? You are not your own; you were bought at a price. Therefore honor God with your bodies.
1 Corinthians 19-20

We are to be baptized as a picture of our new life in Christ.

Therefore go and make disciples of all nations, baptizing them in the name of the Father and of the Son and of the Holy Spirit, Matthew 28:19

Whoever believes and is baptized will be saved, but whoever does not believe will be condemned.
Mark 16:16

We are to meet together regularly with other Christians.

And let us consider how we may spur one another on toward love and good deeds, not giving up meeting together, as some are in the habit of doing, but encouraging one another—and all the more as you see the Day approaching. Hebrews 10:24-25

We are to read and apply the Bible, God's Word.

But He answered and said, "It is written, 'Man shall not live on bread alone, but on every word that proceeds out of the mouth of God.'" Matthew 4:3-4

In Jesus, God's peace will guard our hearts and minds beyond our understanding.

> ***And the peace of God, which transcends all understanding, will guard your hearts and your minds in Christ Jesus.*** Philippians 4:7

His Holy Spirit living inside of us will bear fruit, or show signs of His life within us.

> ***But the fruit of the Spirit is love, joy, peace, forbearance, kindness, goodness, faithfulness, gentleness and self-control. Against such things there is no law.*** Galatians 5:22

Of course there are many other Biblical truths not covered here. Prayerfully follow the Spirit's guidance. He will give you just the right words to say at the perfect time.

> ***For the Holy Spirit will teach you at that time what you should say.*** Luke 12:12

Clean up Before Coming to the Table

How can we get ready for God? I use a word picture I call "The Glove." It is especially effective if acted out. It may be demonstrated with just one person, or you may set up for everyone to try. *Prepare to make a mess and build a memory!*

For each person, you will need:

- One garden glove
- A small container filled with dirt
- A tablespoon
- An empty egg carton
- A small glass of water
- Several very small seeds to plant in each egg carton cup (the smaller the better)
- A towel or newspaper to keep surfaces clean, if needed

For each person, follow these directions:

- Put on the glove. Use only the gloved hand for all of the steps.
- Use the spoon to fill three egg carton cups with dirt.
- Pick up and plant only one seed (about ¼ inch deep) in each of the dirt filled cups using fingers, not the spoon. Be sure to cover the seeds with dirt.
- Pour water from the cup to water each planted seed.

The Mess

Now, use the spoon to fill the fingers of the glove completely with dirt and repeat every step above. It is very difficult to spoon dirt, pick up and plant seeds, and pour out from a glass of water without the hand filling up the glove. It is possible, just not perfect.

The Memory

I am the true vine, and my Father is the gardener.
John 15:1

No one who is born of God will continue to sin, because God's seed remains in them; they cannot go on sinning, because they have been born of God.
1 John 3:9

God the Creator is the Master Gardener. What beauty He created for us to enjoy! He also plants the seeds of salvation into the hearts of His children. As a "glove" we are only a tool that He uses to do His work. He *could* do it without us, but He *chooses* to use us. When we are filled with sin, can He still use us? Yes. Can He use us perfectly? No.

I know that you can do all things; no purpose of yours can be thwarted. Job 42:2

NOTE: Thwart means to ruin or destroy.

We cause things to get messy when there is not room for Him to fill us up, but His plan *will* still be done.

When You Make a Mess,

Ask for Forgiveness and Help

What if we empty that "glove" all the way and ask Him to clean it for us? We do this by asking for forgiveness for anything wrong we have thought, said, or done, and asking for God to clean us and fill us up *all the way* with His Spirit. Once clean, the Master's hand can fully fill up that "glove" and use it to do His work just as He planned—perfectly!

> ***Humble yourselves, therefore, under God's mighty hand, that he may lift you up in due time. Cast all your anxiety on him because he cares for you.*** 1 Peter 5:6-7

God cares for you. He wants to help. Just ask. Ask God to help you understand what He is saying in His Word. With His Spirit of truth inside you, He will guide you and speak to you.

NOTE: If your child has not yet accepted Christ this is still an important step. If you have prayed to make Christ the Lord—Boss—of your life forever, then you will be instrumental in guiding the child to His truth.

> ***But when he, the Spirit of truth, comes, he will guide you into all truth. He will not speak on his own; he will speak only what he hears, and he will tell you what is yet to come.*** John 16:13

> ***The Holy Spirit Whom the Father will send in My name, will instruct you in everything.*** John 14:26

Choose Your Flavor and Serving Size

Pick a verse, section, story, or whole chapter.

***So is my word that goes out from my mouth: It will not
return to me empty, but will accomplish what I desire
and achieve the purpose for which I sent it.***
Isaiah 55:11

***All Scripture is God-breathed and is useful for
teaching, rebuking, correcting and training in
righteousness, so that the man of God may be
thoroughly equipped for every good work.***
2 Timothy 3:16-17

Any Scripture can be used. Just as you serve milk to a baby,
baby food to an infant, and small bites to a toddler, start small
when serving spiritual food to allow your child to comfortably
digest it. Too much at once leaves an uncomfortable feeling, not a
desire for more. There will be times when a "growth spurt"
hungers for further nourishment. Be careful not to miss these
opportunities to serve a larger helping of spiritual food. Move
through the guideline stages in this book as you see your child is
ready.

***Anyone who lives on milk, being still an infant, is not
acquainted with the teaching about righteousness. But
solid food is for the mature, who by constant use have
trained themselves to distinguish good from evil.***
Hebrews 5:13-14

Listen and Answer the Server

After hearing or reading the verse or passage, train your children to always ask the following conversational questions:

- "What is God saying to me?"

- "What do I want to say back to Him?"

We typically teach our children at a very young age to show respect by paying attention when someone is speaking to them and to answer right away. This is a practical way to introduce respect for God as well as relationship with Him. Both are so important.

SECTION FIVE

METHODS AND SAMPLES

The Menu

For the very youngest children, a Bible story or truth is simply read and explained. The child then draws a picture to "give" to God. The verbalized description of the picture is immediately jotted down next to it by the parent or teacher, and then read back to the proud owner.

As reading and writing skills develop, the pages may include more detailed drawings and descriptions, as well as a written prayer response. In addition to the dictated words, the child may also write some sentences independently.

Finally, there will come a time when the entire interaction with the Lord will become private and personal. At this point, the parent need only help the child with their consistency by confirming the date, Scripture, and that something was written. Every so often, the kids may also be asked to choose one journal entry which they are willing to share.

In addition to the growth in developmental skills, there is also an allowance here for personal style and preference. By encouraging your child to use the method he or she prefers, the enjoyment associated with quiet times with God will naturally motivate daily consistency.

All six of my children have found a style for journal writing which they truly enjoy. Before writing this book, I asked each one separately if she or he really likes having a quiet time with journaling. Every single one answered with an emphatic, "Yes!" Yet, when I asked the reason, each one gave a different answer. Use what works!

As they get older, the prayers for younger elementary and older consistently follow a pattern, commonly referred to as "A.C.T.S."

- A = Adoration = "I love You, because…"
- C = Confession = "Please forgive me for…"
- T = Thanksgiving = "Thank You, God, for…"
- S = Supplication = "God, please…"

Write these abbreviations and definitions in the inside cover of each journal as a reminder guide for those working independently. See the samples for the upper elementary and middle school grades.

Additional abbreviations used in the journal samples:

OP = Opening Prayer
(or EOP = Everyday Opening Prayer)

This is prayed silently, not written in the journal. Writing OP simply acknowledges the prayer to "clean up the glove," fill up with the Spirit, and ask for understanding of the Word.

OPL = Ongoing Prayer List (or OL = Ongoing List)

This is a list, which is broken down by categories and written inside the journal cover or on a separate page, which may be used as a bookmark in the journal. In addition to these broad categories, there should be a separate page to add more specific prayer requests.

SC = Scripture Read

List the address or write out key verse(s)

Y = Yesterday and T = Today (or To = Today)

Next to the "Y" on the journal page, write to God how you did yesterday. Make right anything you did wrong. Praise and thank Him for blessings in it.

Next to the "T" on the journal page, write to God what concerns you about today. Give it over to Him and ask for His help to do His perfect will.

P! = Praise! and A = Application

The Kids' Menu

(Write the Date and Scripture on each page.)

TODDLERS AND PRESCHOOLERS

- prayer and verse(s) read by teacher (OP = Opening Prayer)
- picture drawn by child and labels dictated to teacher
- possible activity to go with the Scripture read
- prayer dictated to teacher

YOUNGER ELEMENTARY

- prayer and verse(s) read with teacher (OP = Opening Prayer, A.C.T.S.)
- possible activity to go with the Scripture read
- pictures drawn by child
- labels and prayer written by child with help or dictated to teacher

UPPER ELEMENTARY

- prayer and verse(s) read by child with help only as needed (OP = Opening Prayer)
- optional pictures with or without labels
- prayer response written by child with help only as needed
- optional abbreviated prayer sections (A.C.T.S.)
- optional O.P.L. = Ongoing Prayer List

MIDDLE SCHOOL

- prayer and verse(s) read independently (OP = Opening Prayer)
- optional pictures with or without labels

- prayer response written by teen
- optional abbreviated prayer sections (A.C.T.S.)
- O.P.L. = Ongoing Prayer List
- *Savor the Savior (Pen, Bible, Ice Cream!)*

HIGH SCHOOL

- prayer and verse(s) read independently (OP = Opening Prayer)
- O.P.L. = Ongoing Prayer List
- *Savor the Savior (Pen, Bible, Ice Cream!)*

TODDLERS

AND

PRESCHOOLERS

Kiddie Size, Please!

- prayer and verse(s) read by teacher (OP = Opening Prayer)
- picture drawn by child and labels dictated to teacher
- possible activity to go with the Scripture read
- prayer dictated to teacher

For the youngest children, follow these very easy steps:

- Familiarize yourself ahead of time with the Scripture you will read, so that it can be read with meaning. This is a must.
- Pray a simple opening prayer (OP) out loud, something like this: "Thank You, God, for loving us. Please teach us through Your Word. Amen."
- Holding the Bible, remind them every time, "This is God's Holy Word. That means it is *all* true."
- With the Bible open to the chosen verse(s), read out loud.
- Tell what the verse(s) mean according to the children's level of understanding.
- Say the key verse(s) again. Have the child(ren) repeat part or all of it, so it makes sense.
- Say, "Let's draw a picture for God." Open the journal to the right page, handing a pencil to each child. Be sure to have your own pencil ready. The next steps will be done with only one child at a time.

- The shorter the attention span, the quicker the child will be done. Immediately, say, "Tell me about your picture for God."
- As the child tells about the picture, write down everything onto the page, whether it makes sense to you or not. It will make sense to God. Draw arrows from words that label parts of the picture. Write sentences clearly without writing on top of the artwork.

JOURNAL ENTRY SAMPLES

AGES 2-5

GRAPHICS 1-10

NOTE: All of the journal entries used in this book are used with permission by the six "authors." Names and dates have been removed in order to retain some privacy. In doing so, several Scripture addresses were removed from the samples, but the verses are included in the coordinating comments for each entry. Exact ages have been left off, since the stage and preference is more important to consider when choosing a method that works.

This child told God about the most exciting events of the day—toddler style!

Journal entry verse:

For what I received I passed on to you as of first importance: that Christ died for our sins according to the Scriptures, 1 Corinthians 15:3

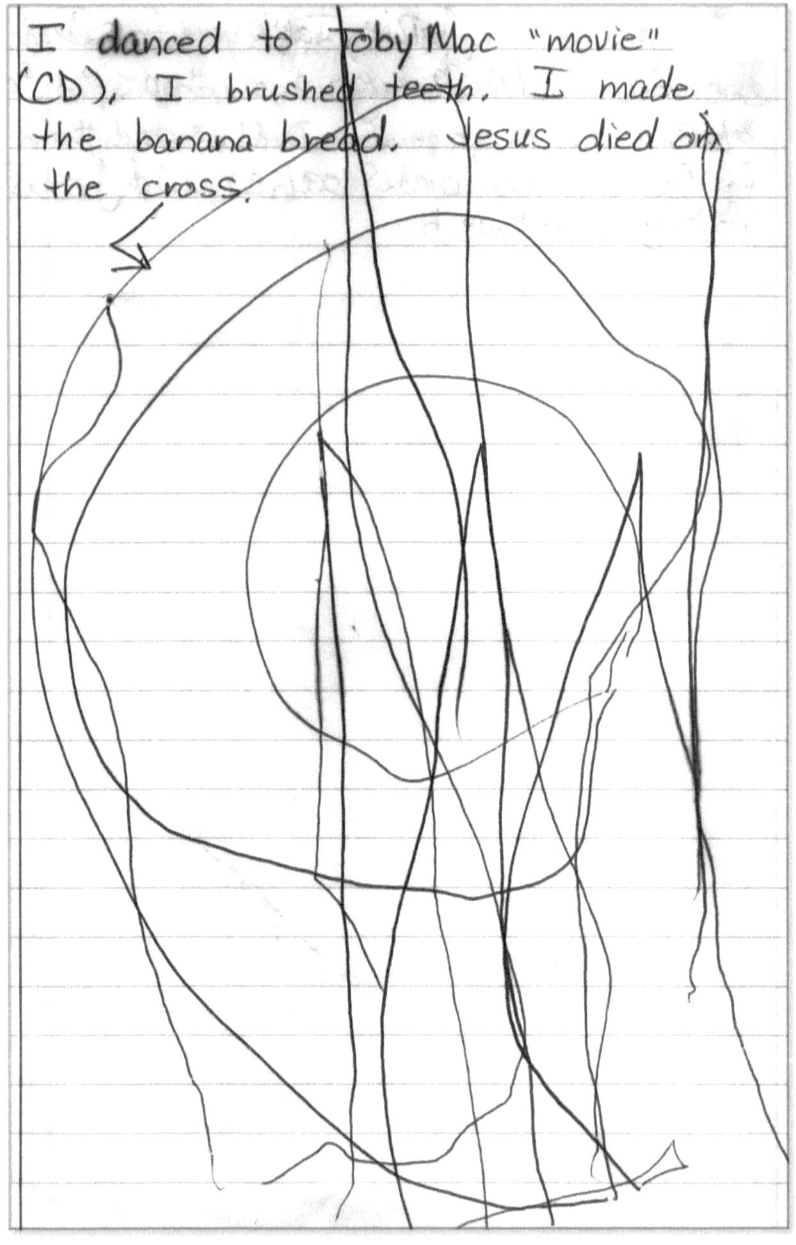

I danced to Toby Mac "movie"
(CD). I brushed teeth. I made
the banana bread. Jesus died on
the cross.

The following two entries were together side by side in the journal notebook using two full pages. Younger kids often need the extra space, which is fine. This was from a large passage of Scripture, which was told with excitement and different voices for the "characters" who spoke. It is a fun one to act out.

Journal entry verse:

This is what happened to Joshua and Caleb:

The LORD said to Moses, "Send some men to explore the land of Canaan, which I am giving to the Israelites. From each ancestral tribe send one of its leaders."

…When Moses sent them to explore Canaan, he said, "Go up through the Negev and on into the hill country. See what the land is like and whether the people who live there are strong or weak, few or many. What kind of land do they live in? Is it good or bad? What kind of towns do they live in? Are they unwalled or fortified? How is the soil? Is it fertile or poor? Are there trees in it or not? Do your best to bring back some of the fruit of the land." (It was the season for the first ripe grapes.)

When they reached the Valley of Eshkol, they cut off a branch bearing a single cluster of grapes. Two of them carried it on a pole between them, along with some pomegranates and figs. That place was called the Valley of Eshkol because of the cluster of grapes the Israelites cut off there. At the end of forty days they returned from exploring the land.

They came back to Moses and Aaron and the whole Israelite community at Kadesh in the Desert of Paran. There they reported to them and to the whole assembly and showed them the fruit of the land. They gave Moses this account: "We went into the land to which you sent us, and it does flow with milk and honey! Here is its fruit. But the people who live there are powerful, and the cities are fortified and very large. We even saw descendants of Anak there. The Amalekites live in the Negev; the Hittites, Jebusites and Amorites live in the hill country; and the Canaanites live near the sea and along the Jordan."

Then Caleb silenced the people before Moses and said, "We should go up and take possession of the land, for we can certainly do it."

But the men who had gone up with him said, "We can't attack those people; they are stronger than we are." And they spread among the Israelites a bad report about the land they had explored. They said, "The land we explored devours those living in it. All the people we saw there are of great size. We saw the Nephilim there (the descendants of Anak come from the Nephilim). We seemed like grasshoppers in our own eyes, and we looked the same to them."
Numbers 13:1-2, 23-33

This is what Moses told the people about it:

When the LORD heard what you said, he was angry and solemnly swore: "No one from this evil generation shall see the good land I swore to give your ancestors, except Caleb son of Jephunneh. He will see it, and I will give him and his descendants the land he set his feet on, because he followed the LORD wholeheartedly."

Because of you the LORD became angry with me also and said, "You shall not enter it, either. But your assistant, Joshua son of Nun, will enter it. Encourage him, because he will lead Israel to inherit it. And the little ones that you said would be taken captive, your children who do not yet know good from bad—they will enter the land. I will give it to them and they will take possession of it. But as for you, turn around and set out toward the desert along the route to the Red Sea." Deuteronomy 1:34-40

Joshua and Caleb told the people they "bringed" the giant grapes from the Promised Land. The people said, "Thank you." They said, "We're too scared." They lived "to the dessert." Joshua & Caleb (Caleb in the Bible is me) believed God. The people stayed in. the dessert.

That's a giant, giant, giant grape.
→

That's Caleb, Joshua, and the bad guy.

The following two entries were together side by side in the journal notebook using two full pages. "The Bob the Tomato Family" was randomly inspired by Veggie Tales.

Immediately Jesus made the disciples get into the boat and go on ahead of him to the other side, while he dismissed the crowd. After he had dismissed them, he went up on a mountainside by himself to pray. Later that night, he was there alone, and the boat was already a considerable distance from land, buffeted by the waves because the wind was against it. Shortly before dawn Jesus went out to them, walking on the lake. When the disciples saw him walking on the lake, they were terrified. "It's a ghost," they said, and cried out in fear.

But Jesus immediately said to them: "Take courage! It is I. Don't be afraid." "Lord, if it's you," Peter replied, "tell me to come to you on the water." "Come," he said.

Then Peter got down out of the boat, walked on the water and came toward Jesus. But when he saw the wind, he was afraid and, beginning to sink, cried out, "Lord, save me!"

Immediately Jesus reached out his hand and caught him. "You of little faith," he said, "why did you doubt?" And when they climbed into the boat, the wind died down. Then those who were in the boat worshiped him, saying, "Truly you are the Son of God."
Matthew 14:22-33

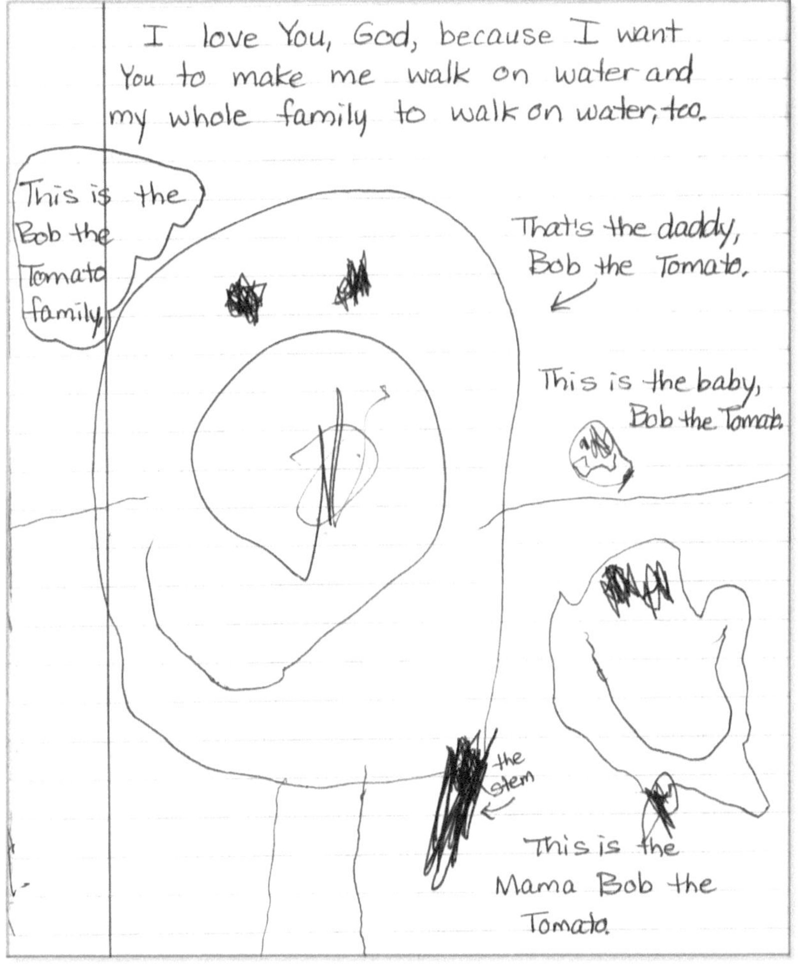

I love You, God, because I want You to make me walk on water and my whole family to walk on water, too.
This is the Bob the Tomato family
That's the daddy, Bob the Tomato.
This is the baby, Bob the Tomato.
the stem
This is the Mama Bob the Tomato.

I did the lightning
God is getting in the sky.
We're just walking on water.
the stem
This is the sister Bob the Tomato.

I don't know what inspired "the sheriff" in the drawing, but these random preschooler additions to the journal pages are often our favorite parts. What a reminder that God sees our hearts and accepts our sincere offerings of praise!

For what I received I passed on to you as of first importance: that Christ died for our sins according to the Scriptures, that he was buried, that he was raised on the third day according to the Scriptures,
1 Corinthians 15:3-4

Lord Jesus,
     I thank You for dying on the cross
and sending Your only Son. I thank You
for helping my heart get joy and
dying on the cross and "rosing" again.
          Amen.

This is Baby Jesus.

"and
a
sherriff

As with the previous entries from a different child about Joshua and Caleb, the following two entries were together side by side in the journal notebook using two full pages. This large passage of Scripture was told with excitement and different voices for the "characters" who spoke. It is a fun one to act out.

See Numbers 13:1-2, 23-33 with Deuteronomy 1:34-40.

These are all the Israelites.
Joshua and Caleb told all the people that they had to go to the Promised Land. The other ten spies said that they didn't want to go. They didn't believe God, and they thought it was too scary. The Promised Land had big grapes, lots of honey, and lots of milk, and giants. The Israelites chose to go in the dessert. When they were old Joshua and Caleb got to see the Promised Land.
God, I will always believe You every day and always pray.
This is a big grape.

Those are all the bad people.
This is the biggest grape in the whole entire world.

Notice the explanation for the new word, "persecution." The prayer shows evidence of the understanding of the verse, which was explained before writing the entry. Also, notice the self-written words. This particular time, the child asked for spelling help.

But I tell you, love your enemies and pray for those who persecute you, Matthew 5:44

Matthew 5:44
"Love your enemies and pray for those who persecute you." (pick on)

God, I will love my sisters and pray for them when they pick on me. aND THaNK YoU FoR MY FAMILY. AMEN

Here are two entries on the same page. The top one shows clear understanding that God will forgive our sins when we ask and mean it. It is apparent from the second entry that this child also understands the command to be baptized.

Verse for the top entry:

If we confess our sins, he is faithful and just and will forgive us our sins and purify us from all unrighteousness. 1 John 1:9

Verses for the bottom entry:

Peter replied, "Repent and be baptized, every one of you, in the name of Jesus Christ for the forgiveness of your sins. And you will receive the gift of the Holy Spirit. The promise is for you and your children and for all who are far off—for all whom the Lord our God will call." Acts 2:38-39

Thank You, God, for this day.
Thank You for the sun and moon and
    stars and the universe.
Thank You for the people You made and
help them to not be sick anymore.
Sorry, God. Will You please forgive
    me for all my sins?
(God will definitely say, "yes.")

Acts 2:38-39

Yes, God, I will get baptized,
because I love You. It will show
everybody that I'm a Christian.
It's a picture of God washing away
my sins. I love You. You are
the nicest person in the universe.
Amen.

YOUNGER

ELEMENTARY

Small Serving, Please!

- prayer and verse(s) read with teacher (OP = Opening Prayer, A.C.T.S.)
- possible activity to go with the Scripture read
- pictures drawn by child
- labels and prayer written by child with help or dictated to teacher

For the younger elementary children, follow these steps:

- Familiarize yourself ahead of time with the Scripture you will read, so that it can be read with meaning. This is a must.
- Pray a simple prayer out loud, something like this:
- *"I love You, God. Please forgive me for anything that I have done to disobey You. Thank You for forgiving me. Please speak to me through Your Word and help me to understand it. Amen." NOTE: This is the Opening Prayer = OP and it follows the A.C.T.S. pattern.*

- Holding the Bible, remind them every time, "This is God's Holy Word. That means it is *all* true."
- With the Bible open to the chosen verse(s), read it out loud.
- Tell what the Scripture means according to the children's level of understanding.
- When appropriate, this is the time to add in an activity which further teaches the Biblical truth from the Scripture

read. Some activities are included with the coordinating journal page samples on the next few pages.

- Say the verse again. Have the child(ren) repeat part or all of it, so it makes sense.
- Have each child open the journal to the right page and take out a pencil.
- Ask, "What do you think God said to you from the Bible today?" Listen for the answers.
- Say, "What would you like to say back to God? Let's make a picture to go with it."
- Wait for each child to draw the picture. Some will also add words to label it or sentences to go with it. Others will only draw the picture.
- With the child next to you (not across), ask, "Would you like to write some of the words, or would you like me to write them?" The answer may change from day to day. Go with it!
- Say, "Tell me about your picture to God."
- Write as the child dictates.
- As the words are written to label parts of the picture, have the child draw the arrows to connect the words to the picture parts.
- Ask, "Is there anything else you would like to say to God?" Write what the child adds on.
- Say, "Let's read what you wrote to God."
- Point to each word as it is read to the child.
- "Now you read it. I'll help if you need it." Point to each word just as you did when you read it. If the child gets stuck, just say the word to keep the flow. This is not typically the best time for sounding out words.
- Encourage enthusiastically! "Great reading! God will *love* your letter and picture you made for Him! "

JOURNAL ENTRY SAMPLES
AGES 5-8
GRAPHICS 11-15

NOTE: All of the journal entries used in this book are used with permission by the six "authors." Names and dates have been removed in order to retain some privacy. In doing so, several Scripture addresses were removed from the samples, but the verses are included in the coordinating comments for each entry. Exact ages have been left off, since the stage and preference is more important to consider when choosing a method that works.

This entry followed an activity that went with the verse. I had ten chocolate Easter eggs for each of the two children next to me.

I said, "Would you like any of my chocolate eggs?"

Both said, "Yes!"

As I handed the candies to them, I told them not to eat them yet. I then offered another and another until each child had ten eggs, and I had none. They noticed this.

"May I have some of my eggs back please?" Both shoved several eggs my way.

I said, "No thank you. I only need the first one back from each of you."

With big eyes and worried faces, each questioned the fairness of this. I then told them that this is what God is saying in Malachi 3:10. I asked them if it is fair for God to ask for just the first one out of every ten, since everything is His. Both were in awe of God's loving generosity, as this entry shows.

Bring the whole tithe into the storehouse, that there may be food in my house. Test me in this," says the LORD Almighty, "and see if I will not throw open the floodgates of heaven and pour out so much blessing that there will not be room enough to store it.
Malachi 3:10

Malachi 3:10 AMEN

God, I love You. so, so much. Thank You very, very much for letting me have nine and letting You have one. AMen

Tithe

God wants the 1st one out of every ten. He gives us nine out of every ten.

This lesson was on praying for Spiritual battles to be won. Notice the understanding of God as Father, or "Dad."

Because you are his sons, God sent the Spirit of his Son into our hearts, the Spirit who calls out, "Abba, Father." Galatians 4:6

NOTE: "Abba" is the familiar term for "Father," like "Dad," implying "my Father."

For our struggle is not against flesh and blood, but against the rulers, against the authorities, against the powers of this dark world and against the spiritual forces of evil in the heavenly realms. Ephesians 6:12

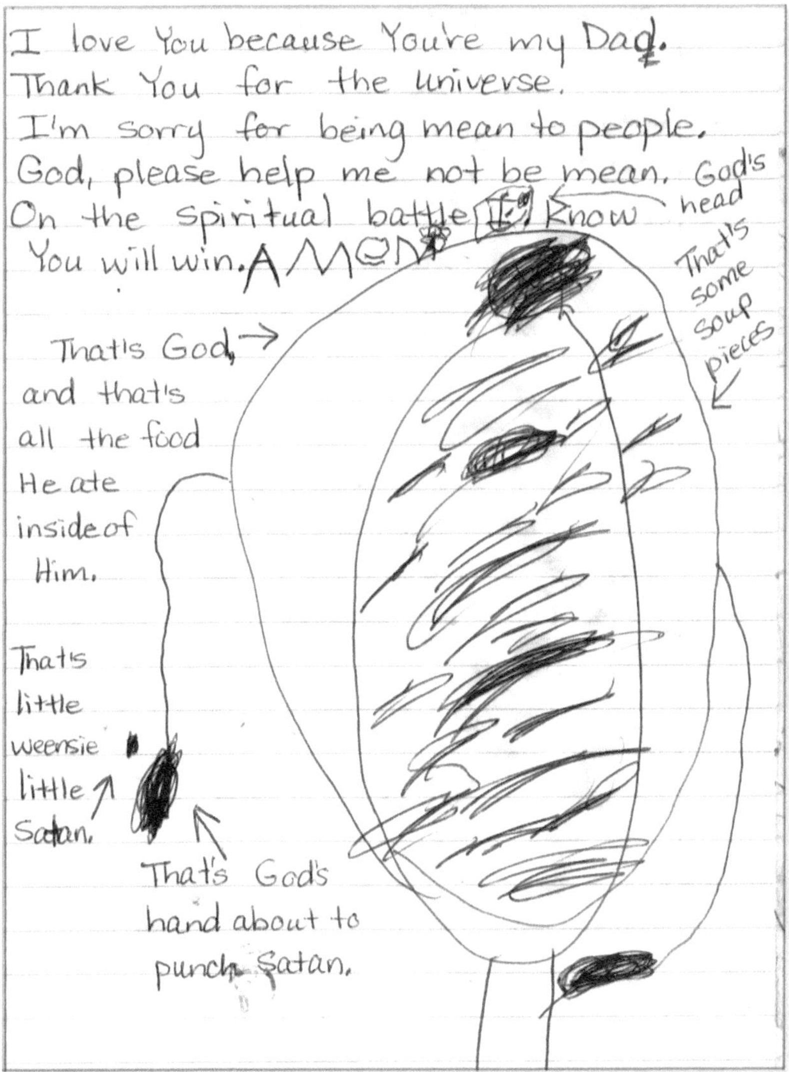
I love You because You're my Dad.
Thank You for the universe.
I'm sorry for being mean to people.
God, please help me not be mean.
On the spiritual battle I know
You will win. AMEN

God's head

That's some soup pieces

That's God, →
and that's
all the food
He ate
inside of
Him.

That's
little
weensie
little
Satan.

That's God's
hand about to
punch Satan.

Note that the misspelled words were not corrected. As long as it can be read, we leave it. The kids know the difference between phonetic spelling and correct spelling. If they ask for help, then I help. If they do not, then phonetic spelling is accepted. I may just make a mental note of a word that is misspelled to do something with it later, but not during journal writing and reading.

This was from a large passage read with great enthusiasm and different voices for the "characters." We also used the pictures from *The Beginner's Bible* storybook, which we read later.

Now the serpent was more crafty than any of the wild animals the LORD God had made. He said to the woman, "Did God really say, 'You must not eat from any tree in the garden'?"

The woman said to the serpent, "We may eat fruit from the trees in the garden, but God did say, 'You must not eat fruit from the tree that is in the middle of the garden, and you must not touch it, or you will die.'"

"You will not certainly die," the serpent said to the woman. "For God knows that when you eat from it your eyes will be opened, and you will be like God, knowing good and evil."

When the woman saw that the fruit of the tree was good for food and pleasing to the eye, and also desirable for gaining wisdom, she took some and ate it.

She also gave some to her husband, who was with her, and he ate it. Then the eyes of both of them were opened, and they realized they were naked; so they sewed fig leaves together and made coverings for themselves.

Then the man and his wife heard the sound of the LORD God as he was walking in the garden in the cool of the day, and they hid from the LORD God among the trees of the garden. But the LORD God called to the man, "Where are you?"

He answered, "I heard you in the garden, and I was afraid because I was naked; so I hid." And he said, "Who told you that you were naked? Have you eaten from the tree that I commanded you not to eat from?" The man said, "The woman you put here with me— she gave me some fruit from the tree, and I ate it."

Then the LORD God said to the woman, "What is this you have done?"

The woman said, "The serpent deceived me, and I ate." Genesis 3:1-13

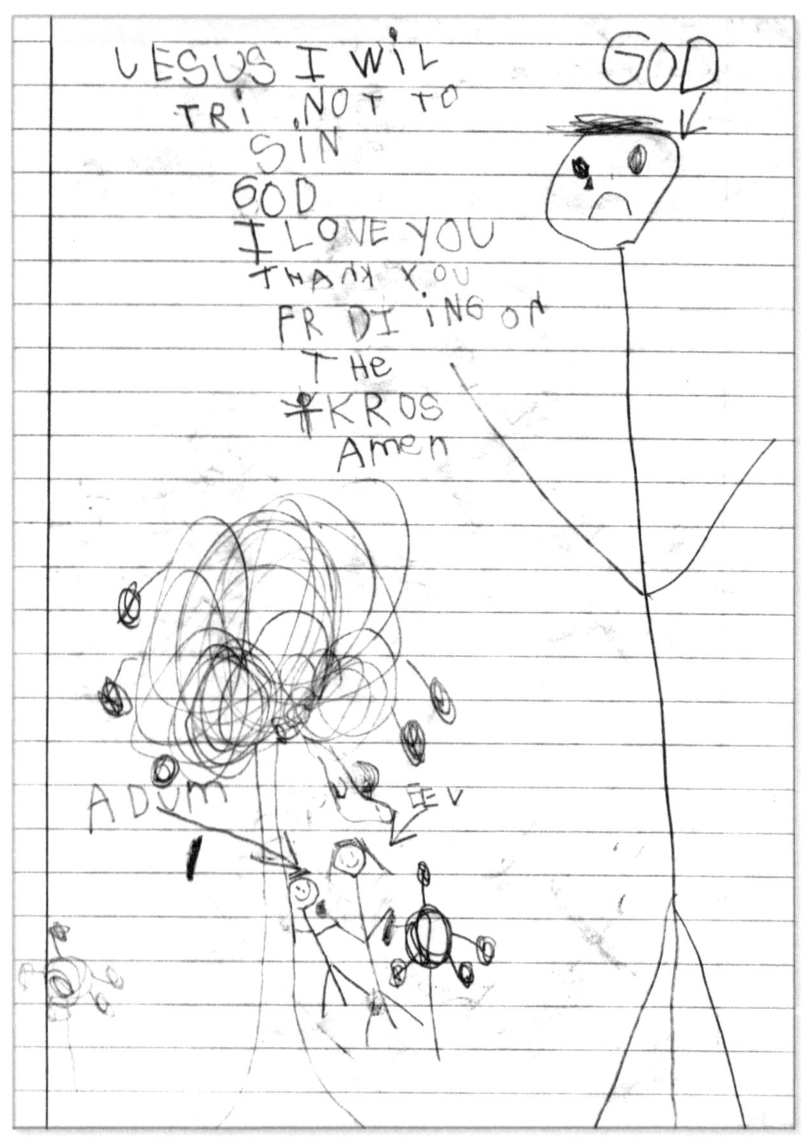
JESUS I WIL
TRI NOT TO
SIN
GOD
I LOVE YOU
THANK YOU
FR DI ING ON
THE
KROS
Amen
GOD
ADOM
EEV

This is another entry from a week when our family was fervently in prayer for victory over spiritual battles. This child understood and chose to fast from eating all sugar for one week to remember to pray often for spiritual battles to be won. This particular entry was written as a result. The lesson had been taught days earlier, but was still of top concern on this day.

For our struggle is not against flesh and blood, but against the rulers, against the authorities, against the powers of this dark world and against the spiritual forces of evil in the heavenly realms. Ephesians 6:12

Dear God I Pray That I will
Not Haf too DIy Goinqto Hevone
I Pray That you Will Win
The Spearichle Badle. I Love
You God Amen.

This is a sample from my child who prefers "vanilla" entries. Note the acknowledgement of Who God is and what God said. Also, notice sentence structure development that was gently learned without drilling. Each day's journal entry is divided by a wavy line.

Ps. 25:1-3 Let my enemies be put to Shame.

9/11/ Ps. 25:4-7 You are my savior.

Ps. 25:8-12

9/12/

You — died on the

mon. Ps. 25:13-15 You —

9/15/

— will Instruct me!

UPPER ELEMENTARY

<u>Medium Serving, Please!</u>

- prayer and verse(s) read by child with help only as needed (OP = Opening Prayer)
- optional pictures with or without labels
- prayer response written by child with help only as needed
- optional abbreviated prayer sections (A.C.T.S.)
- optional O.P.L. = Ongoing Prayer List

With today's technology, many kids are already familiar with instant messaging, texting, and email. What an advantage to teaching written two-way communication with the Lord! You may need to have your children experiment with each style until they find their favorites. They may change from day to day for variety, or stick with one that works. Your kids may even come up with a new combination. Terrific! As long as the journal entry represents two-way conversation between God and the person, it works.

For the upper elementary children, have them choose an option, and follow the steps. It is important that the parent or teacher be readily available if there are any questions about the Scripture, difficult words to understand, how to write something, or if the child wants to share the journal entry.

Plain Vanilla

After the opening prayer and reading the Scripture, think about what God is saying to you, write an "A" for Application/Adoration, and write to God a sentence or a few sentences that show you understand what He just told you. You may even use special handwriting.

Add a Topping

Use the Plain Vanilla method, but in addition to the "A" for Application/Adoration sentence, draw a picture to go with it. You may label the picture or add in cartoon conversations for the drawn characters. Be creative, but make sure it is accurate.

Add Different Toppings

Use the Plain Vanilla method, but instead of just topping it with the "A" for the Application/Adoration sentence, write additional prayers to God. Use any of the letters from A.C.T.S. You may use only one or all of them.

- A = Adoration = "I love You, because…"
- C = Confession = "Please forgive me for…"
- T = Thanksgiving = "Thank You, God, for…"
- S = Supplication = "God, please…"

The Works

Use any combination or all of it together:

- Write out the verse.
- Write out what the verse is saying to you.
- Write your answer to God after you know what He has said to you.
- Draw a picture.
- Label the picture and add comic style words.
- Write the A.C.T.S. prayers.
- Start an Ongoing Prayer List (OPL).

JOURNAL ENTRY SAMPLES

AGES 9-12

GRAPHICS 16-19

73

NOTE: All of the journal entries used in this book are used with permission by the six "authors." Names and dates have been removed in order to retain some privacy. In doing so, several Scripture addresses were removed from the samples, but the verses are included in the coordinating comments for each entry. Exact ages have been left off, since the stage and preference is more important to consider when choosing a method that works.

Each entry represents a different day. Used this way, the "A" may show adoration, application, or acknowledgement of what God is saying. Notice that only one day contains "S" for a request (supplication), but that particular request to memorize the days' verse surely brings adoration to the Author, too.

Job.1   4/14/
A. I Will Praise you No matter
What happens.

Job.2   4/15/
A. Job is sick.

Job.3   4/16/
A. Job is crsing God.

Job.4   4/19/
A. Some people are poor.

Job.5:1-16   4/20/
A. You are asome !!!

Deut. 18:22 4/26/
S. God will you Please help me
Memorize Deut. 18:22?

These entries clearly show a response to having read God's personal communication to the child. Reading it is much like listening to one side of a phone conversation.

Proverbes 10:21-22 4/28/
1. I will hold my lips together when I am thinking somthing bad.

1 Corinthians 10:15-17 4/29/
A. I am part of the body of Christ.

Hebrews 6:13-15 5/2/
A. I want to be a blessing to others.

Proverbes 10:6-7 5/4/
A. I will not be wicked.

S. God please help me to 5/5/
not speak wikedly.

Matthew 5:3-5
A help me to be nice to people who are not nice to me.

Here is the first sample of the A.C.T.S. fully used. Notice that each one finishes the sentence starters for A.C.T.S.

NOTE: This child's sentence starter for "S" was "I ask for…" instead of "God, please…" Both work.

A— You forgive me when I ask. Thank You for doing that.

C— Not doing bible right when I wake up and for not praying that much and for trying to lean on my own understanding. Forgive me. Amen

T— Bringing daddy home safly. Thank you. Amen.

S— You to help me when Daddy goes away for every longer than this time. Please help me with that. Amen

Although a passage was read, one verse was chosen and fully written out. The comic style pictures with words in these entries are excellent to use when teaching other kids. This particular child thoroughly enjoys sharing the journal entries with others, which is a huge benefit to younger siblings, especially. The application in this entry is a letter to God

Dear God, why do I complain? it just makes everyone around me upset. Please help me to make the right choise and sticke with it.
I ♡ U Love,

82

MIDDLE

SCHOOL

<u>Large Serving, Please!</u>

- prayer and verse(s) read independently (OP = Opening Prayer)
- optional pictures with or without labels
- prayer response written by teen
- optional abbreviated prayer sections (A.C.T.S.)
- O.P.L. = Ongoing Prayer List
- *Savor the Savior (Pen, Bible, Ice Cream!)*

Read and follow all of the steps for UPPER ELEMENTARY SCHOOL. In addition, as the student is ready, it is time to move to the companion book, *Savor the Savior (Pen, Bible, Ice Cream!)*. Again, offer a wide variety of choices, and encourage your kids to try new things. Hold them accountable, yet allow their conversations with God to be intimate.

HIGH

SCHOOL

<u>King Size Serving, Please!</u>

- prayer and verse(s) read independently (OP = Opening Prayer)
- O.P.L. = Ongoing Prayer List
- *Savor the Savior (Pen, Bible, Ice Cream!)*

JOURNAL ENTRY SAMPLES
AGES 12-16
GRAPHICS 20-26

NOTE: All of the journal entries used in this book are used with permission by the six "authors." Names and dates have been removed in order to retain some privacy. In doing so, several Scripture addresses were removed from the samples, but the verses are included in the coordinating comments for each entry. Exact ages have been left off, since the stage and preference is more important to consider when choosing a method that works.

From the passage that was read, a focus verse was chosen and written out. A coordinating picture and letter were added in response.

86

ISAIAH 24:1-23
ISAIAH 24:18ᴮ
A— The floodgates of heaven are opened, the foundations of the earth shake.

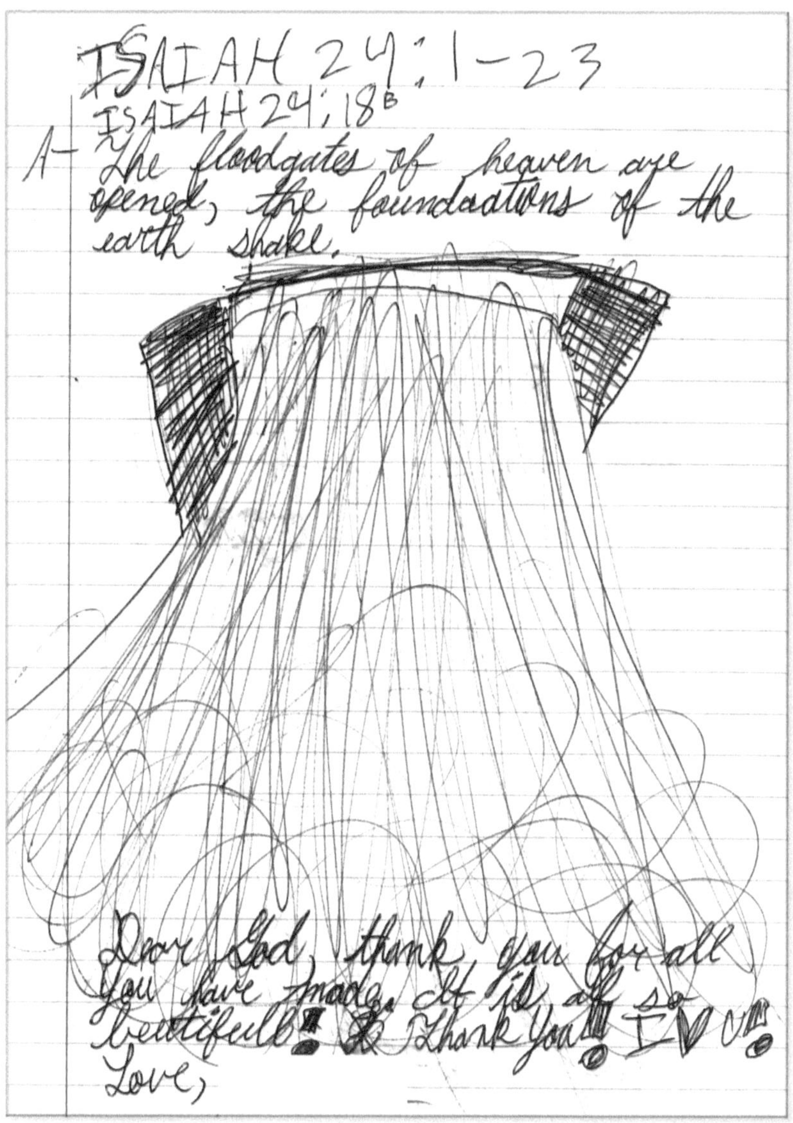

Dear God, thank you for all
you have made. It is, oh so
beautifull! ❤ Thank You!! I ♥ U!!! ☺
Love,

"e.o.p." = "every-day ongoing prayer" and "J.t.t.G." = "Just talk to God." This entry clearly shows A.C.T.S. as well as the creation of new abbreviations.

4/11/
Sc:
Genesis 37

E O P Sc: Genesis 37

A. I ♥ u because: you don't show favoritisom, you love me, you died for me, & you take care of me!

C. I'm sorry for disobeying you.

T. thank you for: takeing care of me every day!

S. I'm praying for: O.L., Daddy, & all who are sick. Amen.

Love,

4/12.
Sc: Matthew 27:27-54

E O P Sc: Matthew 27:27-54

S.t.t.G. I've been amazed at the story, I've never heard it this way before.

Love,

Although the A.C.T.S. letters are not written, this entry shows the progression of each part of prayer. See if you can identify each one: Adoration, Confession, Thanksgiving, and Supplication.

Psalm 34:15-22

dear LORD, thank you so much for taking my place at the cross, and for promising to keep me safe! I'm sorry for taking you for granted sometimes, PLEASE FORGIVE ME. I ♥ U very much! please help me to keep my mind clear and pure, and I pray I would get math done quickly today, and that I woud get writing done even quicker. I ♥ U!

love,

Notice the fancy vine doodling on the "W." This entry obviously was written in response to answered prayer as well as the Scripture.

MATTHEW 4:1-11

Dear LORD, Thank you sooo much for not giving in to temptation and going through all that you did! I can't imagen what it would be like to know that you could have been rescued at any point & Chooseing not to in order to save the verry same people that were hurting and literly killing you. I know I wouden't have gone through it but I Can NOT Thanke you ever enough. I ♥ u! please forgive me for all I'vedone wrong. I'm sorry. Please Thank you sooo much for last night I'm so blessed to know the only loving, and liveing God who will die for His Creations and will use them to bring his other creations to rest in Him and give Him their trust! thank you for useing me last night! I ♥ u! please give   a real friend and give him Confidence and Charecter and trust in you! . . . I ♥ you !!!!   love, love, love,

These next two entries represent the "picture perfect" sundae combination. Everything is there and strategically placed. Note the many abbreviations. See if you can identify each one. You can check your answers with "The Menu."

SC: Romans 5 & 6

OP: Please help me be a peacemaker, reach out & finish all my schoolwork for today,

OI: Jobs, country, starving people, ~~for the~~ Lost to find you, Margin, time w/ family & Daddy, Our church...

TO: I want you to remind me to pray when I wash my hands & get a drink.

P: I don't feel a strong desire for anything any more & I'm content w/ what I have.

A- gracious, savior, perfect, Jesus, righteous, holy, powerful, strong, beneficial, caring, loving...

C- Please forgive my mean comments & flippant remarks, & help me to be kind & submit & not try to control.

T- Thank you for a warm house, food, clothes, Bible, you, my safe environment...

S- Please help me stay content w/ you not this world & to do hard things for you.

I love you,

In addition to the "yesterday" and "today" portions of the entry, a "*" was added for a fervent, heart-felt prayer letter.

SC: 2 Peter 2

OP: Father, please help me to be diligent & get back on track w/ my schedule & eating habits!

OI: family/relationships, friends, home, school, church, needs, wants, desires, dreams, neighbors, your will for me, band & music...

V: Thank you for all the decisions made in VBS!

R: Please help me to continue to be diligent & be ready & rested for tonight!

* God, I don't want to continue to be in sin or go back to my sin. You are righteous, blameless, holy, & persevering. Please make me to be like you. Also I ask for your forgiveness for all my laziness & disobedience & complaining & all my sins. Thank you for allowing me to be a part of VBS & please help me to get on track w/ P.E. & schoolwork & social life. I love you. Please hold me close. -   Amen

This is a picture of the full method from *Savor the Savior (Pen, Bible, Ice Cream!)*.

SC: Proverbs 12

OP: Lord, please forgive me of all my sins. I pray that you would show me your will in what I should save for & whether you want me to go on a mission trip or not & show me what your will is regarding acting, school, & my Job. I trust you & will wait for your answer. Amen

A – Father, you are glorious, righteous, holy, perfect, sovereign, trustworthy, blameless, diligent, protector, & Savior of the world. I trust you to help me w/ all I need. You give me strength & wisdom.

C – Please forgive me for my pride, laziness, procrastination, selfishness, & disobedience. I'm Sorry for Sinning & I pray that you would forgive me & empty me of myself to fill me to overflowing w/ your holy Spirit.

→

T – Thank you for blessing me w/ my family, home, provisions, education, church Job, friends, & for your saving grace. Thank you Lord, for Saving me & loving me.

I Love you,
Love,

S – Lord, I pray that you would help me to be diligent today & get alot done. Also, please show me your will & help me to be productive in the mean time. Your will be done in Jesus' name. Amen.

CONCLUSION

Leaving a Tip

Read these verses about spiritual growth and maturity:

Anyone who lives on milk, being still an infant, is not acquainted with the teaching about righteousness. But solid food is for the mature, who by constant use have trained themselves to distinguish good from evil. Hebrews 5:13-14

Taste and see that the LORD is good; blessed is the man who takes refuge in him. Psalm 34:8

May your kids move from living on "milk" to digesting the "solid food" of His Word each and every day. *Taste and see that the Lord is good!* **Savor the Savior!**

SECTION SIX

QUESTIONS AND ANSWERS

Q: Should my kids journal *every* day?

A: Encourage a *quiet time* with God *every* day. On some days it is not realistic to write very much, if anything at all. On those days, for appropriate ages simply note: the *date*, the *Scripture* read, *silent prayers* to acknowledge unwritten prayer time, and *OPL* to refer to the separate *ongoing prayer list.* The journal record of daily quiet time will show the growing relationship with God. Our Father desires time with each of His children *every* day.

Q: What if my child doesn't *want* to have a quiet time?

A: This is a sticky question, but at our house it is not an option. There will be rare exceptions, just as there are unusual circumstances when one must skip meals. Our minimum requirement is that each of us has a time for quality prayer and to read and understand at least one focus verse for the day. Of course, spiritual food can be snacked on all day long, too, but one can only go so long without any nourishment, either physically or spiritually, before weakening.

Q: Is this only for children who have already accepted Jesus as their Lord?

A: Keep in mind that the Spirit will bring understanding to His living Word. If His Spirit is not yet living within your child, then pray for His Spirit to pour out to draw your child to a point of understanding.

Q: How *long* is this going to take every day?

A: As little or as long as you choose. I sometimes have to set a timer to make certain kiddos break away. As time goes by and the love relationship grows, that time becomes more cherished. The deeper the love, the stronger the desire is to spend time together. *I can promise you this: You will **never** regret your child having spent too much time with the Father.*

Q: What if it is *too* hard for my child?

A: Keep it simple. Try the different methods until you find a variation that works well *for that child.*

Q: Do quiet times *have* to be first thing in the morning?

A: Nope! Pick a time that *regularly* works the best. You may have to experiment to find what works, and it will likely change from season to season depending on your family's schedule. Spending the best time of day with God is key. For our family this is the first thing in the morning, usually before breakfast (or while breakfast is cooking), but sometimes during or after breakfast. Our Father will faithfully meet with His children *every* chance that He can. He is there waiting.

Q: My child hates to write, but loves to text and type on the computer. Could we just *type* something on the computer instead?

A: Sure! As with all quiet time environments, remember to first remove possible temptations that may distract.

Q: Is it okay to do a quiet time while eating?

A: It is completely up to you. Feast with God, or "fast and pray," eating after you are done.

Q: Is this only for homeschool families?

A: Absolutely not. If your kids have to be up extremely early for school, you may need to try different times to find what works, but it is for everyone.

Q: Do your kids really *like* writing in their journals?

A: I actually asked each of my six kids separately in order to be able to answer this question. Every single one (those who love to read and write and those who detest it) answered with a solid, "Yes." Although daily quiet times are "just the way it is" at our house, there are days that the temptation to do something else causes a wrinkled up nose at my predictable question, "Did you do your quiet time?" Ironically, these very often end up as the days when that same child enjoys an especially meaningful visit with God.

Q: *Why* do your kids *like* writing in their journals?

A: Their answers were similar. It is a real way to have a conversation with God like He is a friend sitting right there. Writing to Him after reading what He wrote helps us understand what He is saying. Practicing fancy lettering or special artwork for Him is so fun.

Q: What do your kids love the most about their quiet times?

A: Here are their differing answers: Reading the Bible, special conversations with God, seeing answers to prayers, sharing excitements with Him, writing to Him, reading my old prayer journals—hilarious!

Q: Do your children share their prayer journals for others to read?

A: Very often. As they get older, sometimes they prefer to share a prayer request or praise instead of their intimate conversation with God.

SECTION SEVEN

ENCOURAGEMENT

My prayer for you

For this reason I kneel before the Father, from whom his whole family in heaven and on earth derives its name. I pray that out of his glorious riches he may strengthen you with power through his Spirit in your inner being, so that Christ may dwell in your hearts through faith. And I pray that you, being rooted and established in love, may have power, together with all the saints, to grasp how wide and long and high and deep is the love of Christ, and to know this love that surpasses knowledge—that you may be filled to the measure of all the fullness of God. Now to him who is able to do immeasurably more than all we ask or imagine, according to his power that is at work within us, to him be glory in the church and in Christ Jesus throughout all generations, for ever and ever! Amen.
Ephesians 3:14-21

SECTION EIGHT

TEACHER'S GUIDE

BEFORE DAY ONE

Fellowship fun...

You may have heard that the best way to learn is by involving as many of our senses as we can. These lessons are designed to do just that. Although <u>Savor the Savior for Kids</u> may be used in the privacy of home, outside accountability is ideal to developing this daily routine as a habit. The instructions have been broken down into four, fun lessons with flexibility to do what will work for your particular group. Pick and choose to create the perfect "Son Day" party!

Here are some ideas for setting up the theme for the first class:

- Send out invitations. Be sure to include RSVP details, so you know how many books and supplies to order. Request prepayment if applicable. You may copy the invitation from the back of the book called, "<u>I Scream, 'Son Days Every Day!</u> '"
- Have everyone bring different ingredients for ice cream sundaes.
- Plan to go out for ice cream after the class. (Look for coupons beforehand.)
- Decorate the covers of composition notebooks with scrapbooking paper (maybe in an ice cream theme).

- Granted, everyone cannot eat ice cream, and maybe time will not allow for it. You may want to have everyone draw a picture of the perfect ice cream sundae or make a collage picture of one using glitter and beads and construction paper.

Plan ahead...

Have students pre-buy the <u>Savor the Savior for Kids</u> books so they arrive before the first class. Also, buying the notebooks and all other materials ahead of time will ensure that each student has what is needed for the lesson.

Be sure every person has a Bible. If this is a concern, consider looking at the dollar store or even your local thrift store for extra Bibles. BibleGateway.com is a great resource for printing the Scripture passage that is needed for each lesson. You can then make copies to have available as a *backup* for those who do not have a Bible.

Materials list for each student

- A copy of the book, <u>Savor the Savior for Kids</u>
- One composition notebook
- One pencil with an eraser
- Ink pens in different colors
- Crayons or colored pencils
- Bible

Homework prizes

No matter what the age or stage, prepare to pass out a daily prize to those who did their homework. These will be needed for DAY TWO and DAY THREE. You may also wish to have one for the closing on DAY FOUR for the "victory reward." Here are some prize ideas which you may use for each lesson:

- A variety of pens can be purchased very inexpensively.
- Gum is also inexpensive and comes in sugar free!
- Of course, there is always candy.
- Local restaurants often will donate ice cream coupons.
- All you have to do is ask.
- Be creative, but keep it simple.

Copies and Songs

IMPORTANT: See APPENDIX for optional pages to copy and distribute to each student, as well as RECOMMENDED RESOURCES for songs to download or purchase.

Teacher's Board

For the class, the teacher will also need a white board, dry erase markers (that work), and an eraser.

DAY ONE

Set up...

Ensure that each student has what is needed for the lesson, including:

- A copy of the book, <u>Savor the Savior for Kids</u>
- One composition notebook
- One pencil with an eraser
- Ink pens in different colors
- Crayons or colored pencils
- Bible
- Optional OPL handout (See APPENDIX)
- Homework paper for DAY ONE (See APPENDIX)

Before the students arrive, write the following onto the board:
I Scream, "Son Days Every Day!"

Either pass out copies of the OPL from the APPENDIX, or copy the OPL onto the board for all students to see.

Start with prayer...

Ask the Holy Spirit to guide the lesson and bring understanding. Pray that only the words which are meant to be spoken will be said, according to God's perfect will. Pray for the members of the group; God has each one there for a particular purpose. Pray that He will be glorified by the lesson.

Settle in...

While everyone is getting settled with their materials, and maybe while finishing their ice cream, ask the ice breaker question: ***What is your favorite ice cream and why?*** Don't rush through this first session. It's just the kick-off; so, there will be plenty of time to complete the actual lesson. Take the time for everyone to get engaged as a class.

Subjects for prayers...

Composition notebooks often have spaces inside the front cover for students to list their class information by the day of the week. This is a great place to list basic prayer subjects, which can also be divided by the days of the week. This is called the OPL or Ongoing Prayer List. Here are some general ideas to start with, but take a minute to brainstorm as a class for other prayer subjects that could go with each category:

Sunday – Christians around the world

Monday - Salvations

Tuesday – Families

Wednesday - America

Thursday – Sad and Lonely

Friday – Poor and Sick

Saturday – Special Prayer Requests

Extra prayers may be written on the journal pages.

Super easy seatwork...

Students may either copy the OPL from the white board onto the inside cover of the journal, the first journal page, or a separate piece of paper. If the teacher made copies of the OPL from the APPENDIX, those may be glued inside the front cover or onto cardstock to make a bookmark. It may be kept simple or decorated and even laminated.

Savor the Savior together…

The group will read the title of Section One together from the board:

I Scream, "Son Days Every Day!"

Talk about it! What does it mean?

Why "Scream"?
(Time with Jesus can be really exciting!)

What is a "Son Day"?
(Jesus is God's only Son. Time with Him is a "Son Day.")

Why "Every Day"? We don't go to church every day.
(God wants to spend time with us every day! We can pray and read our Bible—His letter to us—and write a letter back to Him.)

Tune in to teacher-talk…

Teacher, you may use the EvangeCube at this point to explain "God's Invitation" or you may use the following verses. Keep it simple. Do not pray the salvation prayer as a group unless there is individual follow-up to ensure understanding.

> ***Here I am! I stand at the door and knock. If anyone hears my voice and opens the door, I will come in and eat with that person, and they with me.*** Revelation 3:20

This verse is our invitation from God to share His special gift: Himself. Do you ever have friends over for a meal? What do you do while you are all enjoying the food?

Teacher, listen for answers.

Eating with someone is a time of friendship and visiting. God wants to spend sweet time with each of us! You were invited to these "Son Day" parties, but you had to choose to come in to share in the fun, or you would be missing out right now.

How do we "open the door" for God to come in? By answering Him when we understand that He is "knocking" or calling us to Him. *We are to thank Him for buying us the gift of life, ask for His forgiveness for our sins, and then join Him for our life party.*

The Bible says:

> *for all have sinned and fall short of the glory of God,* Romans 3:23

That means every person has thought, said, or done something wrong before. That's what "sin" means. Have you ever thought, said, or done anything wrong before? Have I? What about your parents? We all have, right?

Here is the problem with that: The Bible says that if we sin, then we deserve death. That sure is bad news, but God gives us good news at the same time:

> *For the wages of sin is death, but the gift of God is eternal life in Christ Jesus our Lord.* Romans 6:23

Even though we are supposed to have death because we have done wrong things, God offers us a gift of life forever in Jesus.

> *For God so loved the world that he gave his one and only Son, that whoever believes in him shall not perish but have eternal life.* John 3:16

God loves the whole world so, so much. He knew we would sin; so, He came up with a plan. God came as Jesus, a man, so that He could take our punishment for all of the wrong things we would ever do. Because Jesus was perfect as God's Son, when He died on a cross, His perfect blood covered up all of our sins, washing us and making us perfect and holy like Him. He saved our lives by giving His own life as a free gift, and then God raised Him up to life again after Jesus had been buried for three days. All we have to do is believe this and to say so.

> *If you declare with your mouth, "Jesus is Lord," and believe in your heart that God raised him from the dead, you will be saved.* Romans 10:9

If you don't accept a party invitation, do you get to enjoy the party?

Teacher, wait for kids to answer, "No."

If you don't accept a gift that is given to you, do you get to enjoy the gift?

Teacher, wait for kids to answer, "No."

You also don't get to enjoy life forever with God unless you accept His invitation--His gift.

> *God is faithful, who has called you into fellowship with his Son, Jesus Christ our Lord.* 1 Corinthians 1:9

He wants all of us to have fellowship or friendship with Him through Jesus Christ our Lord. "Lord" means "Boss."

What does "boss" mean?

Teacher, listen for kids' answers.

A boss can be anyone who is in charge of us and can tell us what to do. Have you ever heard anyone say, "You're not my boss!"? We don't like to be bossed by just anyone, do we? What

if we could pick the Perfect Boss who would take care of us in every way? Would you want that kind of boss? That's Jesus!

If you want to have the best life, then choose to let Jesus be the Boss of your life forever. He loves you so very, very much! When you decide to follow Christ as your Lord, or Boss, He gives you another gift as well as life forever with Him.

And hope does not put us to shame, because God's love has been poured out into our hearts through the Holy Spirit, who has been given to us. Romans 5:5

He gives us Himself through His Holy Spirit. The Bible says that God's love is poured out into our hearts through the Holy Spirit, who is given to us. Now, that's a LOT of love!

Teacher, you may now lead the "prayer to accept God's invitation," or you may choose to follow up with each child separately to ensure understanding first.

Prayer to Accept the Invitation

If you understand God's invitation for you to have His free gift of life, then you may pray a prayer to do that. You only need to accept His gift once, because from then on it is already yours; His Holy Spirit lives inside you forever from that point on.

I will say a prayer with you to help you, but it isn't a "magic" prayer that gives you life. It is your belief that God sent Jesus to save you from the punishment for your sins, because He loves you so much. You can then spend your whole life here on earth with Jesus as your Boss and friend. Once you die on earth, you can know without a doubt that you will live in heaven with Him forever and ever. What a Jesus party heaven has ready for all who choose to accept the invitation!

If you are ready, please pray with me. I will say the words first, and then you say them:

- *Lord Jesus, You are God.*
- *I know that I am a sinner, because I do wrong things.*
- *Please forgive me for all my sins.*
- *I believe that You died on the cross for my sins,*
- *...and You rose again.*
- *Thank you!*
- *Please send Your Holy Spirit to live inside of me forever.*
- *You are the Boss of my life forever.*
- *I love You. Amen.*

Top it off – Homework?

Homework for a prize! Give the following assignment and close in prayer.

- Use your OPL to pray every day for each special subject.
- Ask your parents, or another adult you are close to, to read Sections One through Three this week. When they are done, have them sign the homework paper to bring with you to the next "Son Day" party.

DAY TWO

Set up...

Ensure that each student has what is needed for the lesson, including:

- A copy of the book, <u>Savor the Savior for Kids</u>
- One composition notebook
- One pencil with an eraser
- Ink pens in different colors
- Crayons or colored pencils
- Bible
- OPL from DAY ONE
- Homework paper for DAY TWO (See APPENDIX)
- Homework prizes (See *BEFORE* DAY ONE)
- Prizes for "Settle in..." game

Before the students arrive, write this on the board:

(Date)   <u>*Journal*</u>

- *OP = Opening Prayer*
- *OPL = Ongoing Prayer List*
- *SC = Scripture*

In addition, you will need the following items for "The Glove" activity from "Clean up Before Coming to the Table" in SECTION FOUR:

Choose whether you will let one, some, or every kid have a turn. For each person, you will need:

- One garden glove
- A small container filled with dirt
- A tablespoon
- An empty egg carton
- A small glass of water
- Several very small seeds to plant in each egg carton cup (the smaller the better)
- A towel or newspaper to keep surfaces clean, if needed

Pay with prizes…

No matter what the age or stage, quickly pass out a prize to those who did their homework. *(See BEFORE DAY ONE for prize details.)*

Start with prayer…

Ask the Holy Spirit to guide the lesson and bring understanding. Pray that only the words which are meant to be spoken will be said, according to God's perfect will. Pray for the members of the group; God has each one there for a particular purpose. Pray that He will be glorified by the lesson.

Settle in…

Ice breaker game: Ice cream themed "Sit down if…" Everyone stands up to begin. You can play this twice, if time allows. For the first round, the Teacher reads through these statements, and the students sit down if it applies. The last one standing wins. He or she may get a prize *or* get to repeat the game, reading from the bottom of the list up.

Sit down if...

- Plain vanilla is your favorite ice cream.
- You like any plain ice cream better than with stuff in it.
- You don't like nuts in your ice cream.
- You don't like fruit flavored ice cream.
- You eat ice cream at least once a week.
- You don't like any kinds of swirls in your ice cream.
- You would rather go out for ice cream than have it at home.
- You like peanut butter in your ice cream.
- You like chocolate in your ice cream.
- You do not consider chocolate syrup and fudge swirls to be equal.

Subjects for prayers...

See if anyone has thought up any new topics that others may wish to add to their OPL (Ongoing Prayer Lists).

Super easy seatwork...

Each student should copy the sample journal entry from the white board onto the next, fresh journal page.

Savor the Savior together...

Read and follow all directions for "The Glove" activity from "Clean up Before Coming to the Table" in SECTION FOUR.

Tune in to Teacher-Talk...

Teacher, read aloud all of "When You Make a Mess, Ask for Forgiveness and Help" in SECTION FOUR.

Top it off – Homework?

Homework for a prize! Give the following assignment and close in prayer.

- Complete any unfinished homework from last week.
- Every day say your OP (Opening Prayer) to "empty your glove" and "fill it with the Master's hand" by asking forgiveness for anything you have thought, said, or done wrong. Ask God to clean you up and fill you up all the way with His Spirit.
- Use your OPL to pray every day for each special subject.
- On the journal page started today, write the date next to "OP" and "OPL" every day that you say those prayers. BONUS – Write the names of any verses you read next to "SC."
- Ask your parents, or another adult you are close to, to read the first four title sections in Section Four this week. When they are done, have them sign the homework paper to bring with you to the next "Son Day" party.

DAY THREE

Set up...

Ensure that each student has what is needed for the lesson, including:

- A copy of the book, <u>Savor the Savior for Kids</u>
- One composition notebook
- One pencil with an eraser
- Ink pens in different colors
- Crayons or colored pencils
- Bible
- OPL from DAY ONE
- Homework paper for DAY THREE
- A one minute timer will be needed for "Settle In..."

Before the students arrive, write this on the board:

(Date)   <u>*Journal*</u>

- *OP*
- *OPL*
- *SC*
- *ACTS*

Before the students arrive, write this on the board, or make copies from the APPENDIX to hand out:

<u>A.C.T.S. Prayer Starters</u>

- A = Adoration = "I love You, because…"
- C = Confession = "Please forgive me for…"
- T = Thanksgiving = "Thank You, God, for…"
- S = Supplication = "God, please…"

Pay with prizes…

No matter what the age or stage, quickly pass out a prize to those who did their homework. *(See BEFORE DAY ONE for prize details.)*

Start with prayer…

Ask the Holy Spirit to guide the lesson and bring understanding. Pray that only the words which are meant to be spoken will be said, according to God's perfect will. Pray for the members of the group; God has each one there for a particular purpose. Pray that He will be glorified by the lesson.

Settle in…

Play the ice breaker game: "Don't say 'ice cream.'" This can be done as a group or in smaller groups of two or three. One person is the worker, who is to ask the customers how they would like their ice cream served. The customers must then answer as creatively as possible, but no one can say the actual word, "ice cream" or they are out. Set a timer for one minute rounds.

Subjects for prayers…

See if anyone has thought up any new topics that others may wish to add to their OPL (Ongoing Prayer Lists).

Super easy seatwork…

Each student should copy the sample journal entry from the white board onto the next, fresh journal page.

Savor the Savior together…

A.C.T.S. Prayer Starters

- A = Adoration = "I love You, because…"
- C = Confession = "Please forgive me for…"
- T = Thanksgiving = "Thank You, God, for…"
- S = Supplication = "God, please…"

After reading through this chart as a class, test each other. Each person will say a one-sentence prayer, and the others must quickly identify the matching letter: A, C, T, or S. Repeat this without looking at the chart. Continue until all have a solid understanding of what each letter means when used in the prayer journals.

Tune in to Teacher-Talk…

Teacher, read this aloud to the class:

After hearing or reading Bible words, which are God's letters to you, always ask these questions:

- **"What is God saying to me?"**

- **"What do I want to say back to Him?"**

We show respect by paying attention when someone is speaking to us and we are expected to politely answer right away. When we read the Bible, we are reading God's words

to us. We should pay attention and answer politely right away. Since He has written us a letter, we will write Him a letter, too, using our prayer journals.

Top it off – Homework?

Homework for a prize! Give the following assignment and close in prayer.

- Complete any unfinished homework from last week.
- Every day say your OP (Opening Prayer)
- Use your OPL to pray every day for each special subject.
- On the journal page started today, write the date next to "OP" and "OPL" every day that you say those prayers.
- Write the names of any verses you read next to "SC." BONUS – Write one to four prayer sentences using A.C.T.S.
- After reading the day's verse(s), ask the two questions: "What is God saying to me?" and "What do I want to say back to Him?" Write your answers to God in your journal on the page.
- Tell your parents, or another adult you are close to, about the A.C.T.S. prayer starters and what they mean. When you are done, have them sign the homework paper to bring with you to the next "Son Day" party.

DAY FOUR

Set up...

Ensure that each student has what is needed for the lesson, including:

- A copy of the book, <u>Savor the Savior for Kids</u>
- One composition notebook
- One pencil with an eraser
- Ink pens in different colors
- Crayons or colored pencils
- Bible
- OPL from DAY ONE
- Certificate paper for DAY FOUR (See APPENDIX)
- Prizes for "victory reward"

Before the students arrive, write this on the board:

(Date)   <u>*Journal*</u>

- *OP*
- *OPL*
- *SC*
- *ACTS*
- *Y = Yesterday*
- *T = Today*
- *P! = Praise*
- *A = Application/Adoration*

Before the students arrive, copy the POSSIBLE ABBREVIATIONS FOR JOURNAL ENTRIES on the board from the APPENDIX, or make copies to hand out.

Pay with prizes...

No matter what the age or stage, quickly pass out a prize to those who did their homework. *(See BEFORE DAY ONE for prize details.)*

Start with prayer...

Ask the Holy Spirit to guide the lesson and bring understanding. Pray that only the words which are meant to be spoken will be said, according to God's perfect will. Pray for the members of the group; God has each one there for a particular purpose. Pray that He will be glorified by the lesson.

Settle in...

Ask any or all of these questions, either allowing everyone to answer the same one, or taking turns with different questions.

Would you rather...

- Always choose the ice cream flavor for everyone else around you, but never get to eat ice cream yourself, or get to eat ice cream, but never get to choose the flavor?
- Never eat ice cream for the rest of your life, or have to eat ice cream with every meal for the rest of your life?
- Eat ice cream lying down or standing on one foot?

Or for those who want to go a bit sillier...

Would you rather...

- Soak your feet in soft ice cream for 30 minutes, or place a scoop of hard ice cream under each arm pit for 3 minutes?
- Eat ice cream topped with lint or topped with dead ants?
- Would you rather eat a turkey stuffed with ice cream, or ice cream topped with turkey?

You may let students come up with their own, but set the limits right up front.

Subjects for prayers...

See if anyone has thought up any new topics that others may wish to add to their OPL (Ongoing Prayer Lists).

Super easy seatwork...

Each student should copy the sample journal entry from the white board onto the next, fresh journal page.

Savor the Savior together...

Read over the POSSIBLE ABBREVIATIONS FOR JOURNAL ENTRIES from the APPENDIX.

Tune in to Teacher-Talk...

Teacher, read aloud to the class from "The Menu" and "The Kids' Menu" in SECTION FIVE. Also, choose the "serving size" from SECTION FIVE for your group, and read it to the kids. Have them follow along in their books, and be sure to check out the journal page samples to go with it. Encourage open discussion as to what they like or don't like about each style. Find out which method each one plans to use first.

Top it off – Homework?

Give the following assignment, and read the "Teacher's Closure." Close in prayer.

Homework for a prize! Give the following assignment and close in prayer.

- Complete any unfinished homework from last week.
- Every day say your OP (Opening Prayer)
- Use your OPL to pray every day for each special subject.
- On the journal page for each day, write the date, "OP," and "OPL."
- Write the names of any verses you read next to "SC."
- After reading the day's verse(s), ask the two questions: "What is God saying to me?" and "What do I want to say back to Him?" Write your answers to God in your journal on the page.
- Try out different ways of writing in your prayer journal until you find the one that works the best for you. You do not have to only use one method. You might change from day to day.

Teacher's Closure

Teacher, read this aloud to the class:

You did it! Listen to these verses about spiritual growth and maturity:

Anyone who lives on milk, being still an infant, is not acquainted with the teaching about righteousness. But solid food is for the mature, who by constant use have trained themselves to distinguish good from evil.
Hebrews 5:13-14

Taste and see that the LORD is good; blessed is the man who takes refuge in him.
Psalm 34:8

May you move from living on "milk" to digesting the "solid food" of His Word each and every day. *Taste and see that the Lord is good!* Savor the Savior!

SECTION NINE – APPENDIX

WEBSITES AND RESOURCES

"BibleGateway.Com" operated by The Zondervan Corporation, L.L.C. © 1995-2010, The Zondervan Corporation. www.biblegateway.com

"EvangeCube" order online at LifeWay: Biblical Solutions for life, www.lifeway.com/evangecube/

"The Beginner's Bible" by Zonderkidz, the children's group of Zondervan. www.thebeginnersbible.com/

SONGS

Check out these songs (and videos) to add to the "Son Day" party fun:

"**Hosanna**" by Hillsong United; Brooke Fraser, From the Album *All Of The Above.*

"I love Jesus (better than ice cream)" by Terry White and Wanda White, From the Album *The Goads -- One Bad Jam Session*

"Love You More" by Jeff Slaughter, LifeWay 2011 VBS Song, 2010 LifeWay Worship.

"Old Testament (a.k.a The Ice Cream Song)" by Phil Joel, From the Album *deliberateKids 2.*

COPIES FOR GROUP LESSONS

Permission is granted to copy any portions of the following pages in the APPENDIX.

INVITATION FOR KIDS TO JOIN

FOUR SMALL GROUP "SON DAY" PARTIES

I Scream, "Son Days Every Day!"

<u>Savor the Savior for Kids</u> will teach you lots of fun ways to enjoy delicious spiritual food. ***Like creating the ideal ice cream sundae, you will discover the perfect enticing combination to grow in Christ.*** Can you keep from smiling as you eagerly pile on the sundae toppings and then delight in every bite? Just wait for the joy that comes from delighting in the Lord, and then top that with the fruit of the Spirit! Through daily visits with God, you will "Taste and see that the Lord is good!"

FOR:

DATE:

TIME:

PLACE:

RSVP:

MORE INFO:

ONGOING PRAYER LIST AND PRAYER STARTERS

MAY BE GLUED INSIDE JOURNAL COVER

OR USED AS A BOOK MARK

OPL = Ongoing Prayer List

Sunday – Christians around the world

Monday - Salvations

Tuesday – Families

Wednesday - America

Thursday – Sad and Lonely

Friday – Poor and Sick

Saturday – Special Prayer Requests

A.C.T.S. Prayer Starters

- A = Adoration = "I love You, because…"
- C = Confession = "Please forgive me for…"
- T = Thanksgiving = "Thank You, God, for…"
- S = Supplication = "God, please…"

POSSIBLE ABBREVIATIONS

FOR JOURNAL ENTRIES

MAY BE GLUED INSIDE JOURNAL COVER
OR USED AS A BOOK MARK

Additional abbreviations used in the journal samples:

OP = Opening Prayer (or EOP = Everyday Opening Prayer)

This is prayed silently, not written in the journal. Writing OP simply acknowledges the prayer to "clean up the glove," fill up with the Spirit, and ask for understanding of the Word.

OPL = Ongoing Prayer List (or OL = Ongoing List)

This is a list, which is broken down by categories and written inside the journal cover or on a separate page, which may be used as a bookmark in the journal. In addition to these broad categories, there should be a separate page to add more specific prayer requests.

SC = Scripture Read

List the address or write out key verse(s)

Y = Yesterday and T = Today (or To = Today)

Next to the "Y" on the journal page, write to God how you did yesterday. Make right anything you did wrong. Praise and thank Him for blessings in it.

Next to the "T" on the journal page, write to God what concerns you about today. Give it over to Him and ask for His help to do His perfect will.

P! = Praise! and A = Application

HOMEWORK

DAY ONE

Homework for a prize!

- Use your OPL (Ongoing Prayer List) to pray every day for each special subject.
- Ask your parents, or another adult you are close to, to read Sections One through Three this week. When they are done, have them sign this homework paper to bring with you to the next "Son Day" party.

____

Student Name

____

Parent/Adult Signature

____

Prize Given by Teacher

HOMEWORK

DAY TWO

Homework for a prize!

- Complete any unfinished homework from last week.
- Every day say your OP (Opening Prayer) to "empty your glove" and "fill it with the Master's hand" by asking forgiveness for anything you have thought, said, or done wrong. Ask God to clean you up and fill you up all the way with His Spirit.
- Use your OPL (Ongoing Prayer List) to pray every day for each special subject.
- On the journal page started today, write the date next to "OP" and "OPL" every day that you say those prayers. BONUS – Write the names of any verses you read next to "SC" (Scripture).
- Ask your parents, or another adult you are close to, to read the first four title sections in Section Four this week. When they are done, have them sign the homework paper to bring with you to the next "Son Day" party.

____

Student Name

____

Parent/Adult Signature

____

Prize Given by Teacher

HOMEWORK

DAY THREE

Homework for a prize!

- Complete any unfinished homework from last week.
- Every day say your OP (Opening Prayer)
- Use your OPL (Ongoing Prayer List) to pray every day for each special subject.
- On the journal page started today, write the date next to "OP" and "OPL" every day that you say those prayers.
- Write the names of any verses you read next to "SC" (Scripture). BONUS – Write one to four prayer sentences using A.C.T.S.
- After reading the day's verse(s), ask the two questions: "What is God saying to me?" and "What do I want to say back to Him?" Write your answers to God in your journal on the page.
- Tell your parents, or another adult you are close to, about the A.C.T.S. prayer starters and what they mean. When you are done, have them sign the homework paper to bring with you to the next "Son Day" party.

Student Name

Parent/Adult Signature

Prize Given by Teacher

142

HOMEWORK AND PRIZE

DAY FOUR

Homework and a prize!

- Complete any unfinished homework from last week.
- Every day say your OP (Opening Prayer)
- Use your OPL (Ongoing Prayer List) to pray every day for each special subject.
- On the journal page for each day, write the date, "OP," and "OPL."
- Write the names of any verses you read next to "SC" (Scripture).
- After reading the day's verse(s), ask the two questions: "What is God saying to me?" and "What do I want to say back to Him?" Write your answers to God in your journal on the page.
- Try out different ways of writing in your prayer journal until you find the one that works the best for you. You do not have to only use one method. You might change from day to day.
- Enjoy your prize!

____

Student Name

____

Parent/Adult Signature

____

Prize Given by Teacher

Jeri Daniel is available for speaking engagements and personal appearances. For more information contact:

Jeri Daniel
C/O Advantage Books
PO Box 160847
Altamonte Springs, FL 32716

Jeri@knowhisway.org

Please visit the author's website at:
www.knowhisway.org

To purchase additional copies of this book or other books published by Advantage Books call our toll free order number at:
1-888-383-3110 (Book Orders Only)
or visit our bookstore website at:www.advbookstore.com

Longwood, Florida, USA
"we bring dreams to life"™
www.advbooks.com